# Systemic questioning techniques for more success at work

How to learn the art of asking questions step by step and apply It successfully as a coach or manager - including practical examples

Maximilian Seeberg

# CONTENTS

# What you can expect in this book

In professional life, you are constantly faced with situations that present challenges or even develop into serious problems. Teams often end up having lengthy discussions that ultimately fail to produce a truly satisfactory solution. In order to be able to deal with difficulties efficiently, it is therefore very important to have the right communication skills. You can achieve a great deal here with the right questioning technique.

Systemic questions are one such questioning technique. They offer the possibility of obtaining information. However, these questions focus on a change of perspective - changing your own point of view, questioning your own patterns of thought and action and putting yourself in the shoes of other people involved. All of these things enable you to discover new ideas, creative approaches to solutions and a wide range of possibilities for overcoming problems. The questions can be used in various professional areas. For example, in a job interview, when solving customer problems or in the event of disagreements within a team.

In this book you will learn when and how you can use which questions and what advantages the individual questions have. However, using them requires some practice. To prepare you for this, tips and practical examples will be presented later on. In order to understand the meaning of the questions in depth, you will first learn about the theoretical background to questions and communication between people in general.

# What does "systemic questioning" mean?

Systemic questions are a generic term for a special form of questions that have long been used in therapeutic settings or in coaching. However, due to their effect, they are also becoming increasingly important in everyday life and at work. Good communication is now an essential component of successful organizations and companies. But what exactly does "good" mean here? It means that communication is sustainable and effective. Various research findings show that the majority of all wrong decisions are due to a lack of information or misinformation, inadequate processing of information or misunderstandings within communication[1] . To counteract this, a suitable tool of methods is required. One such tool is systemic questions. They can better capture the complexity of processes. At the same time, they bring together the views and people who are important for the process of finding a solution. An answer can then be found together.

Nowadays, managers no longer have to and can no longer keep track of every employee in the department, know everything and decide everything themselves. It is much more important - and this is what they should do instead - to acquire the skills to ask the right questions, listen to the person they are talking to and trigger reflection processes. In this way, they can encourage their employees to develop new perspectives and look at problems from a different angle. This is helpful, for example, in meetings or when a customer

---

[1] cf. Scholer, S. (2017): Leadership in the public sector. Kissing: WEKA Media

complains - generally in situations that drag on for a long time and for which there still seems to be no solution. Here are some examples where systemic questions can be helpful:

- A customer is causing problems and the collaboration is at risk.
- Acquiring new customers is proving more difficult than expected.
- The aim is to collect as much information as possible about an applicant.
- The competition has grown considerably.
- There are interpersonal problems in the college.

This list could go on and on and should serve as a small incentive for you. Can you think of similar situations that are currently causing problems for you, your colleagues or the company?

Without the questions that will soon be presented, it would be difficult and time-consuming to find sufficient information and satisfactory solutions or at least approaches that satisfy everyone involved. The questions help to change the perspective, to think differently and, above all, to think anew. As with everything we start anew, the beginning can be difficult and feel unfamiliar. It is a technique that takes some practice to avoid falling back into old patterns. In the end, however, it holds a lot of potential. It is advisable to approach the questions and their application step by step and first select the questions that are easier to use. These are, for example, circular and solution-oriented questions. Scaling questions can also be used without any problems. These questions are also a good way to start a conversation. As the name suggests, miracle questions and paradoxical questions can leave both you and your counterpart somewhat puzzled if you have not practised using them. But once you have mastered them, they can open up many unexpected opportunities. In any case, it makes sense to first try out the questions in a private setting until you feel more confident with them. You will then be able to deal efficiently with customers and employees as well as with problems and challenges.

Basically, this requires a change in our own communication, because we cannot expect change without also changing ourselves. So take the first step! Your fellow human beings will thank you for it. As an incentive, we will show you some possible advantages of systemic questions:

- Procedural patterns in communication and behavior are broken up.

- Creative solutions come to light.

- Existing resources and potential are discovered and utilized.

- Conversations go round in circles less and are therefore less time and energy consuming.

- The sense of belonging to the company is strengthened as the group dynamic is sparked, everyone involved is part of the whole and solutions are sought together.

Of course, this list is not exhaustive. However, it offers a good insight into what is possible. In order to gain an understanding of systemic issues and the associated communication as well as an idea of the "human system" with its way of thinking and acting, we will now take a look at the theoretical background.

# UNDERSTANDING THE BACKGROUND OF SYSTEMATIC QUESTIONS

In order to understand the basic ideas of systemic thinking and thus systemic questions, it is first necessary to explain some of the concepts of the underlying theories. The concept of autopoiesis, constructivism and second-order cybernetics form the foundation. Perhaps you have heard of one or other of these terms before? Admittedly, they sound abstract. However, they conceal impressive explanations that are essential for understanding the deeper meaning of systemic issues.

The word "autopoiesis" comes from the Greek and was first used in the field of biology. This concept characterizes living systems on the one hand as a process and on the other hand as the ability to maintain or renew themselves continuously and solely from within themselves. Autopoiesis can therefore be translated as "self-maintenance". One example of this is our cells, which continuously reproduce themselves and their components. Furthermore, an autopoietic system is autonomous in relation to its environment, i.e. self-sufficient, but not independent. On the one hand, this means that it decides for itself how it wants to interact with its environment. In this way, it can distinguish itself from the outside world and form its own identity. This approach is called organizational unity. With regard to the cell, it organizes and structures itself independently, but it cannot be completely independent of its environment. It absorbs the things from its environment that it needs to survive. One example of this is the absorption of energy in the form of food. This principle is therefore referred to as "energetic openness". In order to transfer this to the "human" system, we will first look at other models. Firstly, constructivism.

Constructivism is a theory that deals with the question of whether a person can recognize the world as it "really" is. The basic idea of this theory assumes that every person creates their own individual reality - in other words, constructs it. Hence the name constructivism. A person first observes and perceives their surroundings through their sensory organs. For example, they hear a fragment of a conversation and see the reactions of those involved. These stimuli are passed on to the brain and interpreted there so that an image can be formed. Although they have only observed the situation for a few seconds, they think they know what is right and wrong here, how people feel, what they think, etc., and thus evaluate the situation.

However, this interpretation is influenced by the attitudes, knowledge and experiences that people already have within them. The result is a subjective image of objective reality. In this case, the objective reality is the actual course of the conversation. However, no one can say how the conversation really went. Everyone perceives what corresponds to their previous patterns of experience. Everyone interprets situations, conversations and encounters differently. So we can never know exactly why things are the way they are. Every opinion is always just one opinion among many. It is not an objective fact, but always just a subjective possibility. This is how we reduce complexity, as we cannot grasp the "whole of reality", it is too diverse for that. Over time and with every (similar) experience, we develop routines, opinions, ideas and concepts that make everyday life easier. On the one hand, these routines and concepts provide a framework for orientation and make people capable of acting, so we don't have to constantly rethink how we do things. On the other hand, however, this can also create "blind spots". We spend most of our time dealing with things that are important to us, tackling tasks in the way we have always done them because this path has proven to be the most suitable for us so far and has led us to our goal. All of these things usually happen unconsciously and are automatic. They are routines and habits that we have always done. But what are these "blind spots" all about?

From a medical point of view, these blind spots really do exist - they are places in the visual field where the eye cannot see anything. The optic nerve is fused with the retina in these areas. Therefore, there are no photoreceptors here. These receptors receive light stimuli and transmit this visual information to the visual system for further processing. The absence of receptors leads to local blindness, which does not, however, leave a black spot or similar in our field of vision. We see normally, as if the blind spot did not exist. This incomplete information is "filtered out" by the areas of the brain that are responsible for image processing, so that we do not notice the blind spots in everyday life. The partial blindness is therefore not perceived. Neither as something that is there, nor as something that is missing. The philosopher and physicist Heinz von Foerster describes it like this: "We don't see that we don't see." There are some websites on the internet that offer short animations to help you "see" this blind spot. You are welcome to try it out. It's really exciting!

This partial blindness can also be transferred as a metaphor to other areas of life. For example, in the area of observation and communication. As you have just learned, in the sense of constructivism, every observation is dependent on one's own experiences. In this way, everyone arrives at their own subjective observation, which does not depict reality in its entirety or, due to its complexity, is unable to capture it at all. An observation can therefore never be objective.

And this is where 2nd order cybernetics comes in. General cybernetics is originally a scientific field of research that investigates the regulation and control mechanisms of biological, technical or even sociological systems. The focus is on the investigation and the question of what is being observed.

Based on this, 2nd order cybernetics describes the observation of this investigation. The question here is not what is being observed, but how. The observation is viewed from the outside. This can also be described as the meta-level of observation. The purpose of this meta-level is to detect the blind spots described above and make them visible. The problem is not so much that we do not see, it is much more serious that we do not see what we do not see. To put it more simply: that we do not reflect on our thoughts and actions. If we are not aware that we only have our own reality in our heads, which is based on our subjective experiences, and forget that there are other realities, experiences and opinions, we will never be able to understand our fellow human beings and their motives. Instead, if we observe and reflect on our own thoughts and actions, we can also become aware of other realities. Second-order cybernetics invites us to engage with the perspectives of our fellow human beings and opens up their realities.

How can you integrate these theories into your everyday life so that they are of practical use to you? Think about how you can learn about the worlds and motivations of your fellow human beings in a direct way. That's right, by talking to them. Communication is the key word here. The communication models of Watzlawick and Schulz von Thun are therefore presented below.

Paul Watzlawick was an Austrian philosopher, psychotherapist and communication scientist. His model contains 5 so-called axioms, i.e. universally valid rules. You have probably heard the first basic rule of the model before. It reads: You cannot not communicate. This means that communication takes place in every situation. Communication is not only possible on a verbal level, but also non-verbally through behavior and body language.

The second axiom states that every communication has a content aspect and a relationship aspect. The content aspect refers to all the information that one person, i.e. the sender, conveys to another person, i.e. the receiver. How this information is then understood by the receiver depends, among other things, on the relationship between these people. Gestures, facial expressions or tone of voice lend expression to the relationship.

The third axiom describes that communication is always cause and effect at the same time. How and what partner A communicates therefore has an effect on partner B. The latter then reacts to what is said, which in turn is the basis for A's reaction. Communication therefore never has a "real" end point. Even if a conversation ends, similar emotions and thoughts are unconsciously picked up again at the next meeting.

The fourth axiom says that human communication is digital and analog. Digital here means the spoken word, with which information is clearly conveyed. Analog communication involves non-verbal communication. The other person therefore has room for interpretation and can interpret what is said in different ways. This axiom therefore ties in with the first axiom.

The last axiom refers to the level of communication. This can be symmetrical or complementary. Communication is symmetrical when the interlocutors are at eye level. While the focus here is on similarities, in complementary communication it is the differences. These differences exist, for example, in relationships between parents and children, between superiors and employees and between teachers and pupils. Both sides can either use these differences to complement each other, or one is dominated by the other and subordinates itself, which often offers no added value for either side. These axioms summarize some basic findings on interpersonal communication. In particular, they address the aspect of the relationship.

The four-sided model developed by communication psychologist Friedemann Schulz von Thun goes beyond the relationship aspect. In addition to the relationship aspect, a message conveys a factual message, a self-statement and an appeal. Let's take a closer look at the four sides. The factual message of a message is the content information that the sender sends to the recipient. At the same time, every utterance says something about the sender - usually unconsciously. Gestures, facial expressions and tone of voice provide information about the sender's emotions, values and needs. This allows the recipient to sense that there is more to the message than just the content. This also alludes to the relationship level. It shows how the recipient relates to the sender, i.e. what their relationship is like. Here too, posture, tone of voice, wording etc. play an important role. Depending on what the recipient perceives at this level, they may feel respected or patronized, valued or attacked, for example. And this is where the constructivist idea from earlier can also find its place. Our world view, i.e. how we see the world and what "reality" is for us, also determines how a message is received and how we interpret it.

Let's continue with the fourth level, the appeal. With his statement, the sender also wants to ask the recipient to do or refrain from doing something. The appeal can be formulated openly as a request or wish, for example, or it can be placed between the lines and therefore not be obvious or even manipulative.

Every conversation contains these four sides, both when speaking and when listening. The factual level is usually the most straightforward, provided the sender and receiver have comparable knowledge of the topic in question. Misunderstandings can occur if one of the sides is weighted differently by the interlocutors, i.e. if they are each given a different meaning. For example, the sender's primary intention with their statement is to make an appeal to the recipient. However, as the receiver hears primarily with the "relationship ear" due to his personality, his experiences or his rather mediocre day so far, he feels attacked, although this was not the sender's intention at all. There are many reasons why a person hears more in one ear and less in the other. These can be due to socialization, upbringing, experience or background. The receiver's image of themselves and the sender also play a major role. If the recipient has low self-esteem, the relationship ear quickly comes to the fore and they interpret harmless messages as humiliating for themselves. The image we have of our counterpart, whether as a friendly or egotistical colleague, also influences the interpretation of statements.

To summarize these theoretical constructs, they can be summarized as follows: The **concept of autopoiesis** has taught us that a system acts autonomously, but not completely independently of its environment. Humans can also be understood as such a system. According to this concept, everyone therefore decides for themselves who they come into contact with, what they think and how they act. However, as social beings, people cannot be completely independent of their environment. Nevertheless, according to **constructivist thinking,** everyone has their own reality, which is shaped by subjective experiences. Our own reality can therefore never reflect situations as they really are. We are often partially or sometimes even completely blind to other opinions and ideas. It is therefore all the more important that we become aware of this partial view. In the sense of **second-order cybernetics,** we can observe our thoughts and actions, talk about them, reflect on them and change them accordingly. The central element here is communication. According to the **5 axioms**, communication includes both language and behavior. Furthermore, communication is always circular, so it never really has an end and is both cause and effect. In addition, the **four sides of communication** describe how a statement conveys more than just pure information. What I say, and above all how I say it, shows how I feel about the person I am talking to, what I want from them and ultimately says something about me and my personality.

So let's first focus our attention on ourselves, on our filters. Why do we say something the way we say it? Why do we receive what we say in the way we receive it? Everyday messages can be perceived and interpreted differently by each person. They therefore hold a lot of potential - both for positive and constructive cooperation and for misunderstandings or even conflicts. If we observe how we observe and talk about how we talk to each other, we can develop an awareness of these aspects and thus also of our fellow human beings. We will notice differences in the way we look at things and realize which topics we may bring into our communication from our own biography - usually unconsciously.

**Systemic questions** are one way of reaching this meta-level of observation and communication. They open up new perspectives. We can immerse ourselves in the realities of others and try to better understand their thoughts and actions. This is desirable in both private and professional life. In order to counteract interpersonal problems and entrepreneurial difficulties, it is important to no longer view our own reality in isolation, but to place the entire reality - including that of our fellow human beings - in a dynamic context.

Thinking systemically therefore means knowing that the perceptions of all interlocutors are always subjective and that this subjectivity is also reflected in their language and behavior. In order to understand the language and behavior of an individual, we must be aware that everyone is in constant interaction with other actors involved. We therefore find ourselves in a very complex system of different realities. At the same time, however, this also explains that there can be no monocausal explanations and therefore no simple solutions to conflicts and difficulties. Therefore, all those involved must be involved in finding a solution, but according to autopoiesis, we cannot change others in the way that is best for us or that we would like.

As a reminder: an autopoietic system is not completely independent of its environment and must interact with it, for example in the form of food intake.

However, it is so autonomous that it, in this case the human being, decides for itself how it behaves or not. Accordingly, changes in others are primarily possible through "stimuli". These can be achieved, for example, in the form of systemic questions and the associated change of perspective. Ultimately, however, the decision to change behavior lies with each individual. The motivation to do so must come from one's own drive if it is to be sustained in the long term. This is referred to as intrinsic motivation. It is therefore important to ask systemic questions from a meta perspective. This means observing my behavior, my communication and that of my fellow human beings from this very perspective and reflecting on it together with them.

# The variants of
# systemic questions

This chapter introduces you to the systemic questions. They and their respective advantages are described. This will give you an insight into when you can best use which questions. Examples are also given for each question. Remember the theoretical background just explained. You will be able to understand the questions and their wording better if you have the theories in mind. You can also create your own questions for the individual categories that best suit your situation. But don't worry, you can always go back and remind yourself of the theoretical background if you need to. So let's start with the first systemic question.

## CIRCULAR QUESTIONS

The problem described above basically lies in the fact that we always view a situation from the same perspective and with our own understanding of the world or reality and therefore always behave in the same way. Circular questions broaden the interviewee's perspective by including the frequently described realities of third parties. People's behavior is not determined by what others really think about them, but by what they think is thought about them. And it is precisely this third-person perspective that is the focus of circular questions. This is why they are at the heart of systemic questions. They ask about possible assessments of people who "circulate" in the interviewee's environment. These can be, for example, the superior, colleagues or subordinates, as well as people from the private environment, such as the partner or friends. Putting yourself in other people's shoes makes it possible to consider and reflect on their point of view. By thinking "around the corner", you show empathy and understanding for the realities of other people. This can lead to new approaches and ideas.

This is possible both in a conversation with just one person and in the presence of the person whose perspective is being taken. This person can then give direct feedback. It is often only then that it becomes clear why some situations and statements are very personal, hurt the other person and are therefore generally not very helpful. Being aware of such aspects is part of the basis of a trusting and positive working atmosphere. To give you an idea of what circular questions are, here are a few examples. This is how you can ask:

- Put yourself in the shoes of your colleague X. How would he behave in this situation? How would he feel?
- Try to imagine an observer of this situation. What would he observe and what would he say about it?
- If I were to ask your employees what would motivate them, what would they say?
- What would your business partner say if you suggested a change with these consequences?

- If you ask your colleagues what atmosphere prevails in the team, how would they describe it and what would they like to change?

As these questions illustrate, circular questions can be used as an analysis and intervention tool. On the one hand, you can gain information, for example about the atmosphere within the team. On the other hand, the interviewees also make suggestions for improvement, which you can use to introduce appropriate change measures.

If a respondent is unable to answer a question, for example how person X feels about a certain situation, this answer will also provide you with important information. It shows you that no or insufficient thought has been given to the views of other people. If you notice this frequently, you can ask yourself whether your team really feels like a team or whether everyone is just going their own way without paying much attention to the others. This is where team-building measures can be useful. Circular questions also offer other advantages. For example

- The interviewee reflects on themselves and their relationships from a meta-perspective.

- By putting himself in other people's shoes, he can adopt different points of view and perspectives.

- Personally sensitive issues may come to light that should be handled with care in the future.

- In addition, entrenched thought patterns are broken down and new ways of looking at things are introduced, making new approaches to solutions visible and

- the dynamics within a group or among colleagues can be recognized.

At the end of the circular questions, it is important to know that both asking and answering these questions is often unfamiliar. The application requires caution and practice on both sides. In addition, circular questions should not be asked continuously. This often comes across as artificial. Give yourself and your conversation partners time! In the end, processes that prevail in a group can be explored and uncovered.

These newly emerging thought patterns form the basis for change.

## SOLUTION AND RESOURCE-ORIENTED QUESTIONS

When major problems arise, people often unconsciously focus exclusively on them. Thinking is predominantly negative. The bigger the problem, the more negative the attitude of those involved. It is of course important to diagnose the problems in order to be aware of their existence in the first place. However, a purely deficit-oriented approach only reinforces the problem. Breaking out of this cycle is difficult. One option is to ask solution- or resource-oriented questions, which, as their name suggests, focus on the solutions and look at the resources that exist within the team and can be used to overcome the problem. These questions influence the discussions in a positive way. For example, they look at which strategies and options have already been used and which have not yet been discovered and can still be tried out. The overall more positive nature of the discussions also creates a more pleasant working atmosphere in which it is easier for those involved to find solutions. This is precisely what prevents a focus

on the problem. As an example, you can ask the following questions:

- What situations have we already mas-
tered that were similarly difficult?
- How has such a problem been solved in
the past?
- Which approach has proven to be parti-
cularly effective?
- What do we need to ensure that everyth-
ing runs smoothly?
- What skills do we need for the solution?
And who has these skills?
- What other factors are important for suc-
cess?

These questions will help you focus on the positive. Overly negative thoughts block us in our actions.
Everything we think is also expressed in our actions,
which in turn influence our thinking. These questions
have the exact opposite effect. They create a positive
context in which the problem can be tackled in a solution-oriented way.

Further advantages of this type of question are

- The memories of how former difficulties were successfully resolved.
- This reinforces the awareness that solutions are possible and that the team has already successfully overcome difficult phases.
- The focus is on the opportunities and available resources.
- Negative thoughts remain in the background.
- As well as lengthy discussions about the problem. This ultimately leads us to a solution more quickly.

The questions can generate unusual ideas. Every skill is important here and is needed. This also strengthens the team spirit. The positive atmosphere in which everyone is needed is the opposite of the negative cycle of thought. It is about discovering possibilities, talents, people and situations that can contribute to solving the problem.

# HYPOTHETICAL QUESTIONS

"What if"? Hypothetical questions can be summarized in something like this. They are questions directed towards the future. They offer the opportunity to play through new perspectives and solutions in your mind. The aim here is not to find a direct solution to a specific problem, but rather to experiment and evaluate possible ways forward and wishful thinking. The answer to such a question describes theoretically possible situations and their possible solutions or desirable states. There are no limits to creativity here. All ideas that the interviewees have in mind are permitted. It is important to make it clear in advance that everything the participants want to say is welcome. No idea is condemned or ridiculed.

Sometimes it's the unusual ideas that no one has dared to think of before that hold great potential. It is often only then that it becomes clear whether this approach can actually be implemented in practice and makes sense - in other words, whether it can lead to the goal or is more likely to be discarded. But even if the latter is the case, other solutions can be derived from it. This makes it possible to reflect on what changes are possible instead. This hypothetical thinking leads to new insights that would otherwise not have been considered at all. Creative approaches are also important in general professional life. Creative thinking does not necessarily have to involve a problem. If you dare to leave familiar paths and think outside the box, you will see what potential opens up. It is important to ignore limiting thoughts and factors and fully engage in the hypothetical thought experiment. Examples of such questions are

- What would you do if time was no object?
- What would your path look like if you weren't afraid of failure?
- What if you could decide all by yourself?
- What does your dream job look like and what would be important to you?
- What would it mean for you if money were not a limiting factor?

You may realize that these questions are more of a theoretical game and cannot be directly implemented in reality, but they do offer some advantages:

- They encourage creative thinking and promote this ability.
- The next steps can be derived from the answers. New impulses and perspectives are generated.
- Ideas that would otherwise not have come up at all are included.
- They point out possible ways out of dead ends to solve the problem and
- They provide information about the fears and hopes of the respondents.

In summary, hypothetical questions are used to go through and evaluate scenarios in your mind, to analyze and compare ideas. This can be used to evaluate whether and how they can be implemented.

# WONDER QUESTIONS

Miracle questions are a special form of the hypothetical questions just presented. They also lead to new solution scenarios. However, in an extreme form. They are therefore assigned to their own category. In addition, the question focuses on the situation when a certain goal has already been achieved. It helps to go beyond the boundaries of thought and visualize new strategies. In any case, it is more beneficial to focus on wishes, goals and solutions than on difficulties, problems and obstacles. This is why the use of miracle questions can be particularly helpful in muddled and seemingly hopeless situations. Here are some examples:

- Imagine the problem has been solved overnight. How would you recognize it the next day?
- What would change in your life then?
- What does a perfect world look like to you?
- How would you feel if your dream suddenly came true?

As you can see, these questions are about imagining the best possible state. In addition to new ideas, you can also rediscover your motivation and develop positive thoughts and emotions. Further advantages are

- The focus shifts from the problem to solutions and approaches.
- These can be the starting point for the "actual" solution.
- In addition, the answers are not limited by anything. This allows for very creative thinking with correspondingly imaginative results.

Wonder questions are therefore rather abstract, which means that they should always be used in a controlled manner. Mastered here means both practiced and sparing use, because not only can the questions surprise, but the answers can also bring new and interesting perspectives. At the same time, they can stir up the interviewee emotionally. You should be prepared for this, which is why it is important to announce these questions in advance.

# JUSTIFICATION QUESTIONS

We often simply carry out the tasks we are given at work without questioning their exact meaning and purpose, and this is precisely the aim of the justification questions. These questions are intended to make the person you are asking reflect on their actions and at the same time justify them. The motives and thoughts behind why a task was carried out in the same way and not differently can therefore be revealed. The questions can also be used to verify alleged facts or clarify previously limited perspectives on an issue. A one-dimensional approach can thus be analyzed and thus discarded or expanded. Example questions include the following:

- Why do you want to solve the problem in the same way?

- Why are you so convinced of your approach?

- Can you explain your plan in more detail?

- What experiences are you basing your decision on?

- How do you counter objections from your colleagues?
- How did you come to this conclusion?

These questions are not intended to show up the interviewee or to cast doubt on their abilities and achievements to date - on the contrary. As with other systemic questions, the main aim here is to come to terms with one's reality and the resulting way of thinking, acting and working. Conversely, this means putting yourself in other people's shoes and explaining to them why you have chosen this path and are so convinced of your approach. This gives the interviewer a better insight into the interviewee's way of thinking. Other advantages are

- The participants and the team gain a better understanding of certain approaches.
- Reasons for these approaches are also sought and explained.
- This is how one-dimensional views can be recognized
- and any ingrained patterns are questioned and broken up.

Ultimately, this encourages the interviewee to think carefully about their approach. And perhaps this is a good thing. But it can certainly still be optimized, which should be in the interest of all parties involved.

Always choose these questions carefully. As we now know, we can never say for sure how the other person will react to the question and whether they might feel attacked. It is therefore important to make it clear what the aim of these questions is. For example, you may want to optimize certain work processes. An empathetic approach is therefore the top priority when asking systemic questions and when conducting conversations in general. After all, nobody should feel offended.

## SCALING ISSUES

This type of question serves as an initial assessment of problems. They give you an overview of the situation and can reduce its complexity. The use of these questions is therefore particularly useful at times when a problem is particularly complex and its facets seem almost impossible to deal with. They also challenge generalizations and highlight differences in relation to a specific issue. For example, the mood in a team can generally be perceived as poor.

However, when applying the scaling question, they receive different answers. Some give the answers "1" or "2" and thus rate the mood as very bad. However, many also give a "5" or "6", which corresponds to an average value. This illustrates the differences and therefore also the different and above all subjective views. This example once again demonstrates the analysis and intervention function of systemic questions. The information is analyzed here, which makes a significant difference with 1 to 6. At the same time, the question also triggers a process of reflection. The interviewees realize that the mood is mostly okay after all. Nevertheless, there is room for improvement here and, above all, the lower values need to be investigated.

As examples of scaling questions, the classic variant can be listed first. This involves assigning a value on a scale of 1 to 10. 1 corresponds to the weakest and 10 to the strongest.

In addition to this numerical scale, there is also a percentage scale. Here the question can be: "To what percentage are you satisfied with the result?" Or:

"Compared to difficulties you have already solved - where on the scale do you place the current problem?" An extension can then be the formation of an order. For example: "In your opinion, what are the three most important findings from the workshop?" Other scaling questions could be: "How did you manage to go from a 6 to an 8?" or "Why do you think satisfaction dropped from a 9 to a 7?"

Scaling questions offer an easy introduction to a topic and its further processing. Other advantages are

- On the one hand, it encourages self-observation,
- on the other hand, positive and negative changes are quickly recognized and
- They can be used in any situation and do not require much practice.

In situations in which things are difficult to objectify, such as satisfaction, perception or motivation, these can be made "measurable" using scaling questions. In addition, the respondent only has to state a number without having to define it more precisely. Overall, scaling questions make the items surveyed more tangible.

# PARADOXICAL QUESTIONS

These questions are about turning the question into the opposite. Sometimes the wording is very subtle. This is intentional. However, it is important to announce this at the beginning of the interview. The explanations are useful to avoid confusing and overwhelming the interlocutor. Transparency enables greater understanding here. It is important that the other person can get involved in the situation and feels safe as a result. Only then is it possible to deal with negative extremes in your thoughts.

Creativity is also required for these questions. First and foremost, it is not about solving a problem, but rather about what would have to happen to make the problem even bigger and more serious. Paradoxical, isn't it? To illustrate this, here are a few example questions:

- What do you think is causing the project to fail?
- What would completely take away your motivation to work?
- How could the problem be made worse?

- What would have to happen for you to fall out with your colleagues?

- How do you completely sell the new customer?

As you can see, these questions dramatize an existing problem. However, this can put it in perspective and at least partially alleviate the situation. At the same time, however, they also show what should not happen under any circumstances in order to avoid exacerbating the situation.

Other advantages offered by these questions are:

- They can be particularly helpful in deadlocked situations.

- During the conversation, you may also realize that the problem is not as bad as you first thought.

- A baffling question can produce a bafflingly simple answer.

Without a doubt, these questions are characterized by a completely different approach than the previous questions. But in some moments you need exactly that - to see what will not work in any case. Turning the situation around can help you get a little closer to a solution. It never hurts to look at problems from all sides and try to solve them. But this type of question is also more difficult than the others and definitely needs practice.

When dealing with systemic issues, it is important to be transparent in your discussions. Make it clear to the person you are talking to that you are both pulling in the same direction and are interested in finding a joint solution to the problem or improving the situation. Sometimes unusual steps are necessary for this, but they can produce all the more effective solutions. What else you should know about dealing with systemic issues in your day-to-day work will follow shortly. Before that, in the interests of completeness, a few more types of questions are briefly added. However, these will not be dealt with in such detail.

## OTHER QUESTION TYPES

Two other questions that can be categorized as systemic questions are questions about images or metaphors and questions about exceptions.

Questions about images and metaphors appeal to the imagination and emotions. An example of this is:

"Suppose a movie is being made about you - what is the title? Who is in it? How are the roles distributed? What will be shown? And what does the ending look like?" Answering these questions is challenging on the one hand and requires a little more time, but on the other hand they are also fun. They may also reveal deeper longings and desires of the person answering them. Imagination is not only required from him. There are hardly any limits to the creativity of the questioner when selecting and formulating the questions. This can result in ideas that can help the employee questioned or an entire department move forward.

Now let's look at the questions about the exceptions. Some people tend to perceive and describe difficulties as a constant variable. Accordingly, they think and act about their problem in the same way, usually in a negative way. This results in a downward spiral. The problem becomes fixed as unsolvable - just like the person's actions. However, as the saying goes, exceptions prove the rule. And this is where the questions come in. For example, this could be: "Are there days when the employee arrives at work on time?" The answer may indicate that the reason for being late is due to other people, situations or other circumstances. For example, employee X may be a single parent who has moved to a new city and has to take their child to daycare in the morning, which only opens shortly before work starts. The employee does not want to appear disorganized because he has only recently been hired and does not dare to address the situation on his own initiative. A discussion can then be held to find a solution to the problem. You should question generalizations such as "always" or "never" with exceptions. For example with:

- "Really always?" or
- "Really never"?
- "Are there any exceptions?"
- "When are these available?" and
- "What is the reason for the exceptions?"

This allows many problems to be solved quickly.

To conclude this chapter, the closed and open questions are now mentioned. They are not directly part of the systemic questions, but are nevertheless described in order to complete the area.

These questions often serve purely to gain information. Closed questions can be answered with a "yes" or "no". For example: "Have you negotiated the contract with customer X?" Closed questions should rarely be used in an interview, as they put the interviewee under pressure. This can create a feeling of being "interrogated", especially if many of these questions are asked in succession. This creates a negative attitude in the conversation. Rather use them to make targeted decisions or if you want to make sure that you have understood your interviewee correctly in the sense of active listening.

If you are primarily interested in gaining information, open questions are preferable at this point. Start with the "W" question words. In other words, who, what, where, how, when, what for, why, why and so on. This allows the conversation to flow more openly and encourages the interviewee to provide more details. This gives you a greater variety of information.

Please note that the last two questions are primarily aimed at collecting information. This is of course necessary in many respects. However, you should not give the interviewee the feeling of being "interrogated". You should therefore practise using the systemic questions presented. You can now find out what knowledge you still need to use them skillfully and confidently.

# The application of the questions

You now know that these questions exist. We have also described in detail how you can formulate them and what advantages they bring. In addition, you need a certain sensitivity as to when which questions make sense. For example, if you need results in a short time or if a discussion drags on for a long time without results, solution-oriented and scaling questions are suitable. The latter provide an overview of the severity or urgency of a problem, which can then be responded to with further questions, such as solution-oriented questions. They focus on the existing resources and strengths that you can draw on.

If you have a little more time available or are planning a new project, hypothetical questions and wonder questions are often insightful. They lead to creative ideas and new approaches that were previously not considered feasible. Also because they were often not even thought of.

In the case of a deadlocked situation, you can use reasoning questions, paradoxical and circular questions. This involves reflecting on your own actions and looking for sources of error or opportunities for improvement. Paradoxical questions may be confusing at first, but can reveal surprising options. Circular questions offer the opportunity to adopt a different perspective. Looking from a different direction can lead to new impulses and solutions.

However, paradoxical, hypothetical and miracle questions often achieve little or nothing in a short space of time. It is therefore important to know how much time you have available. This allows you to select the appropriate questioning techniques.

In addition to the time available, a certain level of trust is also beneficial. The stronger this is, the more intensively and seriously your conversation partners can engage with the situation and the questions. This ultimately benefits a constructive discussion.

Trust becomes even more important as the complexity of the questions increases. A closed question with a yes-or-no answer or a scaling question does not require as much trust as a miracle question, for example, which can touch on emotions and deeper desires. You should acknowledge the trust placed in you with appreciation and formulate it as such. An open-minded, non-judgmental and empathetic attitude on your part is therefore the basis for such conversations. Overall, your employees will then find their way to you more easily and will not be afraid to ask you for advice, even if they have problems.

Furthermore, it does not always make sense to conduct or even force such an intensive discussion in every situation, as the employee's or colleague's mood and other tasks to be completed also play a key role here. Since a lot of creativity and spontaneity in thinking as well as general openness and trust are required from the interviewee, it is understandable that not every time can be the right time for such a conversation. Therefore, an appropriate sense of timing is also required.

Furthermore, it is not always necessary to have a direct conversation. It may (!) also be sufficient if you (initially) send your questions to your colleagues in writing. On the one hand, this can serve as preparation for the conversation, on the other hand, a written formulation often offers a more intensive discussion of the topic. Of course, this must always be considered on an individual basis and should only be presented to you as another idea. A written record of the conversation can also be used for follow-up and therefore for reflection. Writing down the important content of the conversation creates images that, on the one hand, promote inner self-dialogue, which may even give rise to new ideas, and on the other hand, these images are then better anchored in your consciousness. Further tips are now presented in short form.

## Pay attention to speech signals

During a conversation, pay attention to signals such as volume and body language, tone of voice, eye contact, etc. These give important clues - for example, whether the other person is feeling comfortable or not.

## The length of the question

The shorter the sentences are formulated, the easier they are to understand. This also applies to questions. On the other hand, a longer question leaves more room for narratives and details, which can also be important. At the same time, there is a "danger" of deviating from the actual topic. Your intuition is therefore required here. Think about what your intention is with the question and then choose the appropriate wording.

## Avoid a "question ambush"

Questions that are asked one after the other without interruption exert pressure. The interviewee has hardly any time to think and answer the questions, so they quickly lose their motivation.

## Show interest

Do not withdraw behind the questions, but express y-our serious interest, for example by using phrases such as "I am curious ...", "I would like to know ...", or "I am interested ...". This shows your active participation in the conversation and at the same time takes the pressure off the other person.

## Take breaks

Pauses, which you should include between questions, also help to relieve the pressure. Otherwise, the interviewee will feel pressured and literally run out of air to answer.

## Listen actively

Listening and asking questions belong together. However, not all listening is the same. When you listen passively, what is said is perceived, but you do not give any feedback and may even give a judgmental answer. This should be avoided at all costs and is possible through active listening. For example, include the interviewee's answer in your statement and make sure that you have understood them correctly. You can also incorporate the answer given into your next statement or question. In this way, you put the focus on your interviewee and at the same time show honest interest and responsiveness.

**Avoid leading questions**

By doing so, you indicate the direction in which you would like to hear the answer. However, this does not work in such a conversation and makes the interviewee feel uncomfortable. Such questions contain words such as "nevertheless", "approximately", "probably" etc. An example: "You are also of the opinion that ...". As exceptions prove the rule here too, you can consciously use suggestive questions at appropriate moments - in a humorous and positive way.

Finally, we would like to refer once again to the awareness of the theoretical background of communication and human thought and action. The models of autopoiesis, constructivism and second-order cybernetics as well as the axioms of Paul Watzlawick and the four sides of communication according to Schulz von Thun were presented to you at the beginning. This theoretical introduction was and is not exhaustive, but it does provide an insight into this area. It also provides a sound basis for shaping a conversation in a goal-oriented way and for being able to respond appropriately to the other person's answers.

The following practical examples will show you how to deal with any problematic situations that may arise.

# Examples from practice for practice

This chapter outlines four conversations in which systemic questions are used. A brief description of each situation is followed by the interview excerpt. This is followed by a checklist that you can use to prepare for similar conversations.

# THE JOB INTERVIEW

When you are looking for a new employee, you usually want to find out as much information as possible about the applicant and their skills.

In this example, you would like to know during the interview how the applicant Mr. V. assesses his skills and whether he has ambitions for promotion. So you ask: "Imagine this company is a soccer team. Which position would best suit your skills and where do you see yourself in 5 years' time?" Mr. V. answers: "Well, if I am accepted for this position, I see myself initially in the position of a central player, in midfield or as a striker. On the one hand, I want to have a good overview of the team and also like to keep an eye on the organization and cooperation of the team, on the other hand I want to deliver good results, here in the form of goals. In 5 years' time, I would like to be at least team captain. I still want to be close to the team and actively contribute to its success. I can also imagine becoming the team coach and taking on even more responsibility. I enjoy the contact with management and the resulting combination of theory and practice."

The **metaphorical question** you asked allows Mr. V. to describe his abilities and his desire for development in a creative way. This will give you a diverse insight into his thoughts.

Finally, to find out more about Mr. V's needs and wishes regarding his possible future workplace, ask the following question: "Suppose you could create your perfect working day - what would it look like?" His answer is: "On a perfect working day, I come into the office and meet colleagues in a good mood. I then have various tasks waiting for me at my desk - I prepare the offer for a new customer, then hold an online meeting with them and the contract is signed. I then meet with my team and we discuss the most important things, report on news and successes and work on a new project to which everyone can contribute their strengths. If there was then a great lunch, that would be great!"

What do you deduce from this story? Mr. V. values a good working atmosphere, a variety of tasks, independent and autonomous work, success and an appealing food offer. This says something about his work ethic on the one hand and something about his wishes on the other. The answers to this **miracle question** therefore offer the employer many possible starting points.

Two of the systemic questions have now been presented here and how you can integrate them into an interview. You can give free rein to your creativity. However, there are a few things you should bear in mind. These can be found in the following checklist:

- Which position is the candidate applying for?
- What tasks need to be fulfilled here?
- Is there a lot of customer contact?
- Does the applicant have professional experience?
- What skills and qualities does he or she have that are relevant to the position?
- How does he react in stressful or tricky situations?
- What other information do you need from the applicant?

This list can be extended depending on the position, but it provides basic questions that you can ask during the interview.

# GROWING COMPETITION

A clothing company is beginning to worry because similar companies are getting bigger and bigger and therefore represent serious competition. A meeting between the managing director, Ms. M., and the head of the entire department, Mr. F., is held to find initial ideas.

Ms. M. asks: "On a scale of 1 to 10, how would you rate the growth of us and our competitors over the last 5 years? 1 means no growth at all, 10 is growth that has shot through the roof."

Mr. F. reflects: "I would describe our growth as a 5. It's within expectations, but no more than that. The competition is more like an 8. They are really very successful in some areas."

"You said an average of 5," summarizes Ms. M. "So are there exceptions that go up and down?"

"Hm, yes," says Mr. F. "Our online sales have increased the most. On-site business, on the other hand, is dragging us down. I would therefore make the expansion of online sales the main project for the near future and see if we can scale back the others."

"Why do you want to solve the problem like this?" asks Ms. M.

Mr. F. replies: "On the one hand, because it is not yet clear if and when customers will return to the stores, and on the other hand, because our competitors are only active online and can therefore offer their clothing at more attractive prices. In my opinion, this is also the safer option for the future."

This discussion reveals initial ideas and possibilities that the company can now examine further and implement if necessary. The managing director, Ms. M., incorporated three systemic questions. The first question was a **scaling question**. It was used here for both self-observation and external observation. As a result, differences between one's own company and the competition are directly recognizable. The second question addresses Mr. F.'s answer by asking about **exceptions.** These show which areas have a positive and which a negative balance. Corresponding changes can be derived from this. With the third question, a **justification question,** she finally wants to find out the meaning and purpose of his proposal. He explains the motives for his decision accordingly.

In such situations, it is important to address the prevailing problem. You should therefore consider the following in such conversations:

- What is the current problem?
- What facets or areas does it cover?
- Who are the best contacts here?
- Does it make sense to speak directly with the entire team or with individuals one by one?
- To what extent does the problem affect the mood in the team?
- Can we solve the problem internally or do we need external support?

## FOR PROBLEMS WITH CUSTOMERS

Company K. is a major customer of company S. Recently, company S. has been making late deliveries to company K. The latter has now announced that it will look for another supplier if the deliveries continue to not arrive at the agreed time. Mr. P., the managing director of company S., then meets with the employee responsible for this, Mr. D.

During the conversation, Mr. P. asks him: "What would you do if money were no object?" Mr. D. replies: "If we had unlimited financial leeway, I would hire more employees. The order from K. has been increased in recent months. The time available to us has only been extended minimally. We were able to obtain a very attractive offer and thought we could manage it. But if things go on like this, we'll have to go back into negotiations, which the company will probably not like. But as I said, it would work with more employees." Mr. P. summarizes: "Okay, that means we either need more time or more employees. I remember that you were able to solve a similar problem a few years ago. How did you tackle it?" Mr. D. replies: "Ah yes, you're right. I don't think the K. company will give us any more time. Especially not now, when they have to wait longer for the goods anyway. And you said it - we've already had problems like this in the past. So I would hire more employees - as I did back then. However, they were not hired on a long-term basis. So perhaps we should think about a fundamental expansion. We have the space and the expertise to take on more major customers. What we lack is the manpower in the form of sufficient employees."

**The hypothetical question** posed here first provides the impetus to collect ideas without limiting factors such as money restricting the thoughts. Mr. P. then asks a **solution-oriented question in** order to further specify these ideas and implement them in the real world. On the one hand, it enables Mr. D. to remember a problem that has already been successfully solved. On the other hand, the question directs his attention to possible solutions and points out initial paths that he considers useful for the company.

Problems with customers can occur again and again. In order to solve these as efficiently and, above all, sustainably as possible, you should bear the following things in mind when doing so or in discussions with colleagues:

- Have there been similar problems in the past?
- What was the procedure back then?
- What can you take away from this for the current situation?
- What resources can you activate within the company?
- Which areas or persons should be involved in the discussions?

- What is the cause of the problem and how can it be prevented in the future?

## IN CASE OF DISSATISFACTION IN THE TEAM

The head of department, Ms. C., has recently been receiving a lot of feedback about the bad mood in the team. She wants to get to the bottom of this and therefore invites the employees to individual meetings. She wants to get an overview of the different opinions. During the discussion with employee Mr. E., she asks the question: "Try to imagine an observer who follows what happens in the office throughout the day. What would he see and what would he say about it?"

Mr. E. replies: "He would see that everyone just sits at their desk and works silently. There are hardly any conversations between them. There's no reason to, because everyone does their own tasks and there's nothing to work on together. I don't have the feeling that we are a team. He would also see that we hardly ever laugh or talk about private things. We don't have time for that because there's so much to do. I think the mood has almost hit rock bottom."

Ms. C. gives him the following feedback: "Thank you very much for your openness! There are definitely a lot of things I can work on to improve the mood in the team. What would have to happen for the mood to reach zero?" Mr. E. says: "Oh, yes, I think it would have to continue as before, that simply nothing happens within the team that would make it a team, such as working together on tasks or projects or that we sometimes do activities outside of work."

This answer to the head of department's **paradoxical** question stimulates the employee's creativity, and at the same time he expresses his wishes, which the head of department can simultaneously evaluate as suggestions for improvement . With the **circular question** posed at the beginning, Mr. E. is placed in the meta-perspective of observation. He describes how he perceives the day in the office and the dynamics within the team. This provides Ms C. with many ideas on how to positively influence the mood. For example, she can initiate projects that her employees can work on together, or she offers team days that she leaves up to them to organize. Planning together and spending time outside of work can help employees grow together as a team and enjoy coming to work more.

In the event of conflicts or general dissatisfaction within the team, you should bear the following things in mind during discussions:

- What kind of conflict is it?
- Between which persons does it exist?
- Are individual discussions, a group discussion or a combination of both useful?
- Is there an appropriate relationship between you and the people you are talking to, so that they trust you?
- How have similar conflicts been resolved in the past?

## GENERAL TIPS FOR PREPARING FOR AN INTERVIEW

You now know what questions there are, what advantages they offer and what they can look like in practice. The previous examples have only ever shown a possible section of a conversation. However, implementing them independently can be challenging, especially at the beginning. The following tips will therefore provide you with some guidance on how to prepare and conduct an interview.

The first step is to define the problem precisely. It shows why a conversation is important. The first step is to narrow down the problem. You can think about this:

- What is the problem?
- What effects does it have?
- In what ways are these problematic?
- Who is involved in the problems and should therefore also be included in the discussions?
- Are there any factors that are already standing in the way of solving the problem?
- If so, why and how can these be countered?

It is then important to gain an overview of the overall situation. The problem should therefore be contextualized. This means

- When did the problem start?
- Does it occur in a specific context?
- Are there moments when it doesn't occur?
- Will the problem remain the same or will it change?

- If it changes: under what conditions?

The W questions described above will then help you to narrow down the problem. It only makes sense to talk to the parties involved if the problem is clearly defined. Otherwise, it is very likely to get out of hand and not lead to a constructive result.

The systemic questions are only used once these steps have been completed. Writing down a few key points can be helpful for the discussion. For example, write down points that absolutely must be discussed. You can also make a note of questions that you would like to ask in any case. Here you can think about what type of questions you want to use in order to achieve as much as possible. You already know the advantages of the different questions.

Systemic questions are not a panacea. Rather, they are a way of allowing other, interesting and above all unusual ideas to emerge. They often result in suggestions that can be considered in more detail later on.

In addition to the aspects that you should implement, there are also some that should be avoided. For example:

- Asking too many questions at once and overwhelming the other person,

- have a threatening or sarcastic undertone that already steers the answer in one direction,

- not giving the other person time to answer,

- Asking leading questions or even

- show no empathy or genuine interest in the answers.

# A closing word

The examples clearly show that systemic questions can be very effective. They offer many opportunities to adopt a different perspective and view problems from this perspective. In order for them to be effective, all participants in the discussion should be **willing to break free** from previous and possibly entrenched patterns of thought and action. This results in creative and sometimes surprising approaches. Sufficient **time** is important for this, as well as the freedom and security to approach you with your ideas and wishes without hesitation. This requires an appropriate basis **of trust**.

Certainly, the application of the questions requires practice as well as the knowledge of when which type is best used. The examples just shown, as well as the individual questions presented, provide information on this. For the sake of clarity, the most important tips that you should generally bear in mind when conducting a conversation are summarized here.

- Be aware of the theoretical background of human thought and action as well as the basics of communication (chapters 2.1 and 2.2).
- Be sensitive to the choice of questions and the timing of an interview. This requires practice and patience.
- Therefore, give yourself and your conversation partner time.
- A sustainable use of systemic questions also requires empathy and active listening.
- This goes hand in hand with paying attention to non-verbal signals.
- It can be useful to announce systemic questions, for example in the case of paradoxical questions.

- Use more open questions than closed questions to gather information.
- Note the effect of written answers to questions. Use them for preparation and/or follow-up.

In conclusion: ask more questions overall and thus maintain communication within your team. This will enable you to recognize difficulties at an early stage. Often, serious problems don't develop from this in the first place. And if they do: use the questions for brainstorming in order to be successful together.